With Love from The Gossip Girl Cookbook

Enjoying Your Favorite Dish with A Little Bit of Side Talk

by

Betty Green

Copyright © 2021 by Betty Green. All Rights Reserved.

Copyright/License Page

This book is under a license which means no one is allowed to print a copy, republish it or sell it. Also, you are not allowed to distribute the content from inside this book. The only one who has permission to do these things is the author. If you came across an illegal copy of this book please deleted it immediately, if possible contact us and get the legal version.

This is a book for information and the author won't take any responsibility for the actions that the reader takes following this info. The author has done his part to check that everything inside the book is accurate. So every step that the reader follows must be done with caution.

Table of Contents

Introduction 5

Chapter I - Main Course Recipes 6

    Recipe 1: Spaghetti 7

    Recipe 2: Brioche Sandwich 9

    Recipe 3: Broiled Salmon 11

    Recipe 4: Waldorf Salad 13

    Recipe 5: Sushi 15

    Recipe 6: Eggs Benedict 18

    Recipe 7: Yogurt Rice 21

    Recipe 8: Ham with Cherries 24

    Recipe 9: Borscht Soup 26

    Recipe 10: Pumpkin Pie 29

    Recipe 11: Big Bowl of Salad 32

    Recipe 12: Leftover Casserole 34

    Recipe 13: Mashed Potatoes 36

    Recipe 14: Buttery Beans 38

    Recipe 15: Fried Chicken 40

    Recipe 16: Truffle Grilled Sandwich 42

Chapter II – Drink Recipes 44

    Recipe 17: Cosmopolitan 45

    Recipe 18: Cognac Cocktail 47

    Recipe 19: Gin Martini 49

    Recipe 20: Blue Lagoon 51

    Recipe 21: Vitamin Fruit Cocktail 53

Chapter III – Dessert Recipes 55

    Recipe 22: Humphrey Waffles 56

    Recipe 23: Blair's Macaroons 58

    Recipe 24: Dessert Crepes 61

    Recipe 25: Muffins 63

    Recipe 26: Danish Pastry 65

    Recipe 27: Serena's Croissants 67

    Recipe 28: Strawberries and Cream 69

    Recipe 29: Madeline Cookies 71

    Recipe 30: Vanessa's Candies 73

Conclusion 75

Announcement 76

About the Author 77

Introduction

If you love Blair and what she stands for, you will fall head over heels in love with these delicious and sassy recipes too. Whether you are invited to one of their foodie trips or looking to recreate one at home, we have got your back.

The show was about teenage varsity girls and how they formed an alliance around food, parties, and relationships. In this book are 30 recipes from the series. We have even added Blair's thanksgiving pie, Rufu's waffles, and everything sweet, sour, salty, crunchy, and flaky in between.

If you have a party and looking for the perfect theme and recipes, you just found it.

Enjoy!!

xxxxxxxxxxxxxxxxxxxxxxxxxxxxxxx

Chapter I - Main Course Recipes

xxxxxxxxxxxxxxxxxxxxxxxxxxxxxxxxxxxxxx

Recipe 1: Spaghetti

Lily and Rufus decide to have a dinner date at the latter's home. They go for spaghetti with homemade sauce. Easy to make, this is sure to please your guests.

Yield: 2

Total Prep Time: 30 minutes

List of Ingredients:

- 30 oz. tomatoes
- 2 tbsp. olive oil
- 1 medium red onion, chopped
- 2 tsp. garlic, minced
- 1 cup basil leaves
- 1 lb spaghetti
- ½ cup Parmesan cheese, grated
- Salt and pepper to taste

xxxxxxxxxxxxxxxxxxxxxxxxxxxxxxxxxxxx

How to Cook:

1. Add the tomatoes to a mixer and blend till smooth.

2. Add the oil to a saucepan and toss in the onions and garlic and sauté.

3. Pour in the tomatoes and season with salt and pepper.

4. Cook on medium heat until the sauce thickens.

5. Meanwhile, boil a pot of water and add in the spaghetti.

6. Once complete, drain and add to the sauce.

7. Roughly tear the basil leaves and add to the dish.

8. Sprinkle parmesan on top and serve hot.

Recipe 2: Brioche Sandwich

Serena and Blair are often seen carrying a brioche sandwich to school. The gang, in general, love their sandwiches and eat them quite often. Here's one that you will love!

Yield: 2

Total Prep Time: 20 minutes

List of Ingredients:

- 5 tbsp. cheddar cheese, grated
- 5 tbsp. Gruyere cheese, grated
- 1 tbsp. parsley
- 1 tsp. mustard
- 1 garlic, minced
- 4 brioche buns
- 2 tbsp. butter
- Salt and pepper to taste

xxxxxxxxxxxxxxxxxxxxxxxxxxxxxxxxxxxxx

How to Cook:

1. Add the cheddar, Gruyere, parsley, garlic and mustard to a food processor and blend.

2. Apply a thick layer of the mixture over the bread slices and sprinkle salt and pepper.

3. Heat a griddle and add in the butter.

4. Press down the bread slices and cook till the bread turns crispy.

5. Serve hot.

Recipe 3: Broiled Salmon

Another delicacy served at Bart's brunch is broiled salmon, which tastes just as delicious as it looks!

Yield: 4

Total Prep Time: 20 minutes

List of Ingredients:

- 4 salmon fillets
- 5 tbsp. olive oil
- 1 lemon, juice and zest
- 2 tbsp. sugar
- 2 tbsp. soy sauce
- 2 tsp. parsley
- 2 tsp. thyme
- 1 tsp. garlic, minced
- Salt and pepper to taste

xxxxxxxxxxxxxxxxxxxxxxxxxxxxxxxxxxx

How to Cook:

1. Add the oil, sugar, soy sauce, lemon juice and zest to a bowl along with the parsley, salt, pepper, garlic and thyme and mix.

2. Add in the salmon fillet and rub the mixture.

3. Lay the salmon on a greased baking tray and pour the oil mixture on top.

4. Broil in a preheated broiler for 15 minutes.

5. Serve with a sprinkling of parsley leaves on top.

Recipe 4: Waldorf Salad

A tribute to Blair Waldorf and her rich lifestyle. Created by a chef at the Waldorf Astoria hotel, this salad is world-famous and a favorite among celebs.

Yield: 2

Total Prep Time: 15 minutes

List of Ingredients:

- 1 tbsp. lemon juice
- 5 tbsp. mayonnaise
- 2 apples
- 1 cup grapes
- 4-5 lettuce leaves
- 1 cup celery
- 1 cup walnuts, toasted
- Salt and pepper to taste

xxxxxxxxxxxxxxxxxxxxxxxxxxxxxxxxxxxx

How to Cook:

1. Core and slice the apples.

2. Cut the grapes in half and thinly slice the celery.

3. Add mayonnaise to a bowl along with the salt, pepper and lemon juice and mix.

4. To assemble, add the lettuce to the bowl and sprinkle apple, grapes and celery on top.

5. Pour the mayonnaise all over and serve.

Recipe 5: Sushi

Blair and Nate meet at a Chinese restaurant and order Sushi. Blair is quoted as saying once men have a taste of Caviar, I don't know how they can settle for catfish. But you don't have to worry about either as this recipe uses crabmeat and tuna!

Yield: 2

Total Prep Time: 30 minutes

List of Ingredients:

For rice

- ½ cup Sushi rice, cooked
- 3 oz. rice wine vinegar
- 1 tbsp. sugar
- 2 tbsp. mayonnaise
- 1 tbsp. soy sauce

For sushi

- 5-6 nori sheets
- 1 small cucumber
- 5 tbsp. crabmeat, cooked
- 1 can tuna
- 1 red pepper
- 1 spring onion
- 1 avocado
- 1-inch ginger

xxxxxxxxxxxxxxxxxxxxxxxxxxxxxxxxxxxx

How to Cook:

1. Mix the rice wine vinegar, sugar, soy sauce and mayonnaise in a small bowl.

2. Cut the cucumber, pepper, crab meat, tuna, avocado and ginger into thin strips.

3. To make the rolls, layout bamboo mats and line them with nori sheets.

4. Add the vinegar to a small bowl and dip your fingers.

5. Pick up a tbsp. of rice and pat it down in the center of the sheet.

6. Drizzle the vinegar mixture all over the rice.

7. Place the tuna, avocado, spring onion or crab meat in the center.

8. Starting from the side closest to you, start rolling the mat and tightly.

9. Press it down and gently unravel.

10. Cut into circles and serve with soy sauce.

Recipe 6: Eggs Benedict

If there is one thing Chuck loves apart from Scotch, it's Eggs Benedict. You too will fall in love with this dish, and so will your family!

Yield: 4

Total Prep Time: 30 minutes

List of Ingredients:

For Hollandaise

- ½ cup butter
- 2 egg yolks
- 2 tsp. lemon juice
- ¼ tsp. paprika
- Salt and pepper to taste

For eggs

- 6 eggs
- Salt to taste
- 1 tbsp. vinegar

For Benedict

- 6 slices bacon
- 2 English muffins
- 1 tbsp. butter
- 5 tbsp. chives, chopped
- 1 tbsp. dill, chopped

xxxxxxxxxxxxxxxxxxxxxxxxxxxxxxxxxxxx

How to Cook:

1. To make the sauce, add butter to a pan and heat till foamy.

2. Join the egg yolks and water to a blender and whizz till smooth.

3. Pour in the butter and blend.

4. Pour the lemon juice and paprika and toss in salt and pepper.

5. Pour into a bowl and set aside.

6. Boil water in a medium-sized pot and pour in vinegar and salt.

7. Once it boils, crack open an egg and add it to the water.

8. Allow it to cook gently and rise to the top.

9. Repeat with the remaining eggs.

10. Add the bacon to a pan and cook for 5 minutes or until crispy.

11. Place the English muffins in the same pan and toast for 5 minutes or until toasted.

12. To assemble, half the muffins and apply a thick coat of butter on both sides.

13. Place a slice of bacon followed by the poached egg and spoon the hollandaise.

14. Serve warm with a sprinkling of chives and dill leaves on top.

Recipe 7: Yogurt Rice

Blair and her minions are always spotted eating yogurt. Safe to say it is their favorite food to maintain their barbie-like figure. Here is a dish inspired by the same.

Yield: 4

Total Prep Time: 30 minutes

List of Ingredients:

For rice

- 2 ½ cups water
- 1 cup rice
- 2 cups yogurt
- ½ cup milk
- ¼ cup carrots, grated
- 2 tbsp. cilantro, chopped
- 2 green chilis, chopped
- 5 tbsp. pomegranate seeds
- Salt and pepper to taste

For seasoning

- 1 tbsp. oil
- 1 tsp. mustard seeds
- ½ inch ginger, minced
- 10 curry leaves
- 2 red chilies, chopped

xxxxxxxxxxxxxxxxxxxxxxxxxxxxxxxxxxxx

How to Cook:

1. Soak the rice in water for 10 minutes and add to a pressure cooker. If you don't have one, add it to a pot of boiling water.

2. Cook until the rice is soft.

3. Add the milk and yogurt to a bowl and along with the chilies, salt and pepper and mix.

4. Add in the grated carrot, pomegranate and the rice.

5. Mix until everything is well combined.

6. Add oil to a small skillet and toss in the mustard seeds, ginger, curry leaves and chilies.

7. Once the mustard starts to splutter, pour it over the rice and mix.

8. Serve with a sprinkling of cilantro leaves on top.

Recipe 8: Ham with Cherries

Chuck's father, Bart, holds an annual brunch for his foundation. Lavish food is served on well-decorated tables with champagne being poured into glasses and strawberries dipped into cream. The main attraction at the brunch is ham with cherries.

Yield: 4-6

Total Prep Time: 1 hour 30 minutes

List of Ingredients:

- 6 lb ham
- 1 cup cherries
- 1 tbsp. brown sugar
- 1 tsp. cumin powder
- 1 tsp. cinnamon powder
- 1 tbsp. horseradish
- 1 lemon, juice and zest
- Salt and pepper to taste
- ½ cup water

xxxxxxxxxxxxxxxxxxxxxxxxxxxxxxxxxxxx

How to Cook:

1. Clean and place ham on a baking dish and use a sharp knife to score a criss-cross pattern all over.

2. Add the water to the bottom and bake in a preheated 350 Fahrenheit oven for 45 minutes or until cooked.

3. For the cherry glaze, add sugar, salt, pepper, horseradish, cinnamon, salt, lemon juice, zest and cumin to a pan and bring to a boil.

4. Pour it over the ham and stud the cherries into the cuts at equal distances.

5. Place in the oven for 15 minutes.

6. Carve and serve.

Recipe 9: Borscht Soup

Dan frequents a Ukrainian restaurant, which serves up a lot of delicacies. One among them is borscht, a delicious soup made with beetroots and pork.

Yield: 4

Total Prep Time: 1 hour

List of Ingredients:

- 2 large beetroots, shredded
- 2 carrots, shredded
- 15 oz. pork sausage
- 3 potatoes, chopped
- 1 tbsp. oil
- 5 oz. tomato puree
- 1 cup water
- 1 cabbage, shredded
- 2 tsp. garlic, minced
- Salt and pepper to taste
- 4 tbsp. cup sour cream
- Parsley to sprinkle

xxxxxxxxxxxxxxxxxxxxxxxxxxxxxxxxxxxxx

How to Cook:

1. Heat a skillet and crumble the pork.

2. Keep stirring until it browns.

3. Boil water in a medium pot.

4. Add the sausage along with the beetroot, potatoes and carrots and cook till soft.

5. Add in the cabbage and tomato puree and mix.

6. Add oil to a small skillet and toss in the onions and garlic.

7. Sauté till brown.

8. Pour it into the pot and toss in salt and pepper.

9. Cover and cook for 10 minutes.

10. Serve hot with a drizzle of sour cream and a sprinkling of salt and pepper.

Recipe 10: Pumpkin Pie

Dan and Serena plan to spend Thanksgiving with their parents and Blaire decides to make Harold's famous pumpkin pie. Here is a recipe for the same.

Yield: 4

Total Prep Time: 50 minutes

List of Ingredients:

- 10 tbsp. butter
- 2 cups flour
- 1 tbsp. sugar
- ½ tsp. baking powder
- 4 tsp. vinegar
- 1 egg yolk
- 1 cup cold water
- 1 cup pumpkin puree
- 2 tsp. allspice
- 2 tsp. paprika
- Salt to taste

xxxxxxxxxxxxxxxxxxxxxxxxxxxxxxxxxxx

How to Cook:

1. For the dough, add the flour, salt, baking powder to a bowl and mix.

2. Add the egg yolk, vinegar and water to another bowl and mix.

3. Remove and add the flour into the egg mixture.

4. Add in the butter and knead a firm dough.

5. Wrap in film and refrigerate for 40 minutes.

6. Add to a floured surface and roll out to fit an 8-inch pie dish.

7. Flute the edges and save for later.

8. Blind bake the crust for 10 minutes in a pre-heated 350 Fahrenheit oven.

9. Add the pumpkin puree to a bowl along with the all-spice, paprika, salt and pepper and mix.

10. Pour into the pie base and use the excess dough to cover the pie.

11. Bake in a preheated 350 Fahrenheit oven for 45 minutes and serve.

Recipe 11: Big Bowl of Salad

Yet another common sight during feasts, a bowl of salad is always present at the table. The Humphreys go for simple salads while the Waldorf and Van Der Woodsen go for lavish ones.

Yield:

Total Prep Time: 50 minutes

List of Ingredients:

- 1 medium squash
- 2 tbsp. honey
- 2 tbsp. olive oil
- 6 oz. baby spinach
- 5 tbsp. pomegranate seeds
- 1 medium apple, chopped
- ¼ cup parmesan cheese, grated

xxxxxxxxxxxxxxxxxxxxxxxxxxxxxxxxxxxx

How to Cook:

1. Half the squash and place on a greased baking tray.

2. Bake in a preheated 400 Fahrenheit oven for 50 minutes.

3. Cut into cubes.

4. Add the honey and olive oil to a bowl and mix.

5. Season as per your taste.

6. To assemble, add the squash, apple, pomegranate and spinach to a bowl and pour the dressing all over.

7. Sprinkle the cheese on top and serve.

Recipe 12: Leftover Casserole

The thanksgiving on the last season of the series captures elements from all the previous seasons. While recalling the past, Blair and her mother are seen digging helping themselves with thanksgiving leftovers.

Yield: 6-8

Total Prep Time: 45 minutes

List of Ingredients:

- 2 cups cranberry sauce
- 2 cups mashed potatoes
- 2 cups turkey, shredded
- 2 cups corn
- 1 ½ cup turkey gravy
- ¼ cup milk
- 3 cups stuffing
- ½ cup broth

xxxxxxxxxxxxxxxxxxxxxxxxxxxxxxxxxxxx

How to Cook:

1. Add the shredded turkey, potatoes and cranberry sauce to a bowl and mix.

2. Pat it down into a baking dish and sprinkle corn all over.

3. Mix the gravy and milk and pour over the corn.

4. Mix the stuffing and broth and pour.

5. Bake in a preheated 400 Fahrenheit oven for 45 minutes.

6. Cut and serve.

Recipe 13: Mashed Potatoes

No thanksgiving is complete without mashed potatoes. It plays an important role be it a lavish thanksgiving dinner at the Waldorf household or a humble affair at the Humphreys.

Yield: 6

Total Prep Time: 40 minutes

List of Ingredients:

- 4 lb potatoes
- 5 tbsp. butter
- ½ cup milk
- 5 tbsp. sour cream
- Salt and pepper to taste

xxxxxxxxxxxxxxxxxxxxxxxxxxxxxxxxxxxx

How to Cook:

1. Boil water in a deep pot and add in potatoes.

2. Cook until soft.

3. Add the milk and butter to a pan and bring to a boil.

4. Peel and mash the potatoes.

5. Pour in the milk mixture and mix.

6. Add in the sour cream, salt and pepper and mix.

7. Serve hot with thanksgiving turkey.

Recipe 14: Buttery Beans

Yep, you guessed it. Another delicious looking plate of food served at Bart's brunch, butter beans with lemon wedges is the perfect dish for vegetarians among you.

Yield: 4

Total Prep Time: 30 minutes

List of Ingredients:

- 1 lb green beans
- 1 tbsp. garlic, minced
- 2 tbsp. butter
- 1 lemon
- Salt and pepper to taste

xxxxxxxxxxxxxxxxxxxxxxxxxxxxxxxxxxxx

How to Cook:

1. Add the beans to a skillet and pour in water to cover them fully.

2. Bring to a boil and simmer for 10 minutes.

3. Drain the beans and add them to a plate.

4. Add the butter to a pan and toss in the garlic, salt and pepper and toss in the beans.

5. Coat fully before squeezing lemon over it.

6. Serve hot.

Recipe 15: Fried Chicken

Fried chicken is always on the table at the Humphrey Thanksgiving, placed right next to the turkey. You and guests will enjoy this recipe!

Yield: 10-12

Total Prep Time: 45 minutes

List of Ingredients:

- 2 whole chicken
- 5 cups flour
- 1 tbsp. garlic, minced
- 1 tbsp. onion powder
- 3 tsp. paprika
- 2 cups buttermilk
- Oil for deep frying
- Salt and pepper to taste

xxxxxxxxxxxxxxxxxxxxxxxxxxxxxxxxx

How to Cook:

1. Cut the chicken into pieces, you can ask your butcher to do it.

2. Add the flour, pepper, salt, garlic, onion powder and paprika to a bowl and mix.

3. Add the buttermilk to a large bowl.

4. Preheat the oil for frying in a large pot.

5. Start by dipping the chicken into the buttermilk and roll it around in the flour mixture.

6. Gently lower into the pit and fry for 15 minutes or until the inner flesh is cooked.

7. Allow it to cool a little before serving with a dip of your choice.

Recipe 16: Truffle Grilled Sandwich

In a pilot episode, Serena and Chuck are seen sharing a sandwich which, of course, is very fancy. It's a grilled sandwich with truffle oil and here's a recipe.

Yield: 4

Total Prep Time: 30 minutes

List of Ingredients:

- 2 bread slices
- 1 cheese slice
- 1 small onion, sliced
- 2 tbsp. butter
- 1 garlic, minced
- 2 tbsp. truffle oil
- Salt to taste

xxxxxxxxxxxxxxxxxxxxxxxxxxxxxxxxxxxx

How to Cook:

1. Add oil to a pan and toss in the onions.

2. Add them to a bowl once they turn golden.

3. Mix the butter and garlic.

4. Apply a thick coat of butter to both sides of the bread.

5. Place it in the same pan and press it down.

6. Toast until brown on both sides.

7. To assemble, place the onions followed by the cheese slice and drizzle truffle oil.

8. Sprinkle salt, cover the bread and place on a hot pan.

9. Serve once the cheese melts.

Chapter II – Drink Recipes

xxxxxxxxxxxxxxxxxxxxxxxxxxxxxxxxxxxxxx

Recipe 17: Cosmopolitan

It goes without saying that the girls on the show love their Cosmos! They are often spotted with a Cosmopolitan, chit-chatting and gossiping away!

Yield: 1

Total Prep Time: 5 minutes

List of Ingredients:

- 2 oz. vodka
- ¼ ounce triple sec
- ¼ ounce cranberry juice
- ¼ ounce lemon juice
- 2 small ice cubes
- Lemon twist

xxxxxxxxxxxxxxxxxxxxxxxxxxxxxxxxxxxx

How to Cook:

1. Add the lemon juice, cranberry juice, triple sec and vodka to a shaker and shake for 30 seconds.

2. Fill ice cubes in a glass and pour in the drink.

3. Serve with a lemon twist on the glass.

Recipe 18: Cognac Cocktail

Blair is obsessed with Chuck and Chuck is obsessed with scotch. It's a strange love triangle as Chuck is always seen nursing a glass of Scotch. Here's a classic scotch cocktail for your party.

Yield: 1

Total Prep Time: 5 minutes

List of Ingredients:

- 5 oz. lemon juice
- ½ oz. lime juice
- 2 oz. Cognac
- ½ tsp. sugar
- Orange peel twist

xxxxxxxxxxxxxxxxxxxxxxxxxxxxxxxxxxxx

How to Cook:

1. Add the lemon juice, Cognac, lime juice and sugar to a shaker and shake for half a minute.

2. Add ice cubes to a glass and pour the drink.

3. Serve with an orange twist.

Recipe 19: Gin Martini

The go-to drink for Serena and Blair, Gin Martinis are spotted quite often on the show. Easy to make, they are perfect to get the party started.

Yield: 1

Total Prep Time: 5 minutes

List of Ingredients:

- 3 oz. gin
- 1 oz. Vermouth
- 1 dash orange bitters
- 2 Olives

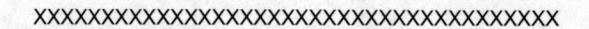

xxxxxxxxxxxxxxxxxxxxxxxxxxxxxxxxxxxx

How to Cook:

1. Fill ice cubes in a glass and pour in the gin and orange bitter.

2. Pour the vermouth and stir for half a minute.

3. Drop in the olive and serve.

Recipe 20: Blue Lagoon

In one of the episodes, Serena is spotted sipping on a blue lagoon. Easy to make, your guests will be instantly attracted to this cocktail!

Yield: 1

Total Prep Time: 5 minutes

List of Ingredients:

- 1 oz. Vodka
- 1 oz. Curacao
- 2 tbsp. lemon juice
- Ice cubes
- Cherry

xxxxxxxxxxxxxxxxxxxxxxxxxxxxxxxxxx

How to Cook:

1. Add ice cubes to a tall glass.

2. Pour in Curacao and vodka and stir.

3. Add in the lemon juice and mix.

4. Drop in the cherry and serve.

Recipe 21: Vitamin Fruit Cocktail

Vitamin water is the go-to drink for nearly all the characters on the show. Safe to say they switched up regular water with vitamin-infused water and you should do the same!

Yield: 1

Total Prep Time: 15 minutes

List of Ingredients:

- 2 blackberries
- 1 kiwi
- 1 orange
- ½ inch ginger
- 2 mint leaves
- 15 oz. water

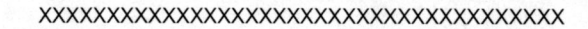

xxxxxxxxxxxxxxxxxxxxxxxxxxxxxxxxxxx

How to Cook:

Half the berries, mince the ginger and thinly slice the kiwi and orange.

Add the water to a pitcher and drop in the fruits.

Add the mint leaves and use a muddler to lightly bash everything.

Add to tall glasses and serve.

Chapter III – Dessert Recipes

xxxxxxxxxxxxxxxxxxxxxxxxxxxxxxxxxxxx

Recipe 22: Humphrey Waffles

The Humphreys are often seen having waffles at their household. Rufus is always serving his kids delicious-looking waffles. Once you have a taste, you will make it a staple at your house too!

Yield: 8

Total Prep Time: 30 minutes

List of Ingredients:

- 1 cup flour
- 4 tbsp. sugar
- 1 tsp. cinnamon powder
- 2 eggs
- ½ cup butter, melted
- 3 tsp. baking powder
- 1 ¾ cups milk
- 2 tsp. vanilla extract
- Maple syrup to drizzle
- Strawberries to sprinkle

xxxxxxxxxxxxxxxxxxxxxxxxxxxxxxxxxx

How to Cook:

1. Sift the flour, sugar, baking powder and cinnamon.

2. Separate the eggs and add the whites to a bowl and blend till stiff peaks.

3. Add the yolks to another bowl along with the milk, oil and vanilla and whisk till well combined.

4. Add in the egg whites and gently fold them in.

5. Add the flour mixture and fold in.

6. Preheat a waffle iron and add a tsp. of butter.

7. Pour a ladleful of the batter and close.

8. Place on heat for 5 minutes each side or follow manufacturer instructions.

9. Serve with a drizzle of maple syrup and strawberries on top.

Recipe 23: Blair's Macaroons

Blair is obsessed with Macaroons! She is often seen biting into delicious-looking, colorful macaroons while soaking in her luxurious bathtub. You too can experience the same by trying out this recipe.

Yield: 10-12

Total Prep Time: 40 minutes

List of Ingredients:

For macaroons

- ¼ cup sugar
- 3 egg whites
- 2/3 cup sugar
- 1 cup almond flour
- 2-3 drops green food color

For vanilla buttercream

- 3 cups powdered sugar
- 1 tsp. vanilla extract
- 1 cup unsalted butter
- 3 tbsp. cream

xxxxxxxxxxxxxxxxxxxxxxxxxxxxxxxxxx

How to Cook:

1. Add the egg whites to a bowl and beat till stiff peaks form.

2. Add in sugar and fold the mixture.

3. Mix the sugar and almond flour.

4. Fold it into the egg whites and add 2-3 drops of green food color.

5. Add a tbsp. of the mixture into a piping bag and pipe 2-inch circles on a lined baking tray.

6. Allow them to stay for an hour or until they form a hard skin.

7. Bake in a preheated 285 Fahrenheit oven for 10 minutes and cool.

8. For the buttercream, add the sugar, vanilla, butter and cream to a bowl and whisk until light and fluffy.

9. Once the macaroons cool, add 2 tsp. of the cream in the center and sandwich with another macaroon.

Recipe 24: Dessert Crepes

Dessert Crepes are present on the table during most brunches, feasts and dinner parties. These sweet delights are sure to woo guests and family members.

Yield: 6-8

Total Prep Time: 30 minutes

List of Ingredients:

- 3 tbsp. butter
- 1 cup flour
- 5 tbsp. sugar
- 4 eggs
- 1 ¼ cup milk
- Powdered sugar to sprinkle
- Strawberries to sprinkle

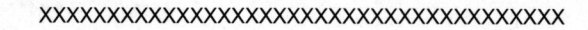

xxxxxxxxxxxxxxxxxxxxxxxxxxxxxxxxxxxx

How to Cook:

1. Break the eggs into a bowl and pour in the milk.

2. Whisk and add in flour, butter and salt.

3. Heat a medium skillet and add a tsp. of butter.

4. Pour a ladleful of the mixture and use the back of the ladle to spread it.

5. Cook for a minute or two on both sides and serve with a sprinkling of powdered sugar and strawberries.

Recipe 25: Muffins

As we know, Blair and Serena love to attend brunches, parties and feasts. A common feature among the spread are muffins, placed on well-decorated cupcake stands. You too can place these muffins on a fancy stand for your party.

Yield: 12 muffins

Total Prep Time: 40 minutes

List of Ingredients:

- 2 tsp. baking powder
- 2 cups flour
- 1 cup sugar
- 1 egg
- 3/4 cup milk
- 1 tsp. vanilla extract
- 5 tbsp. cup vegetable oil

xxxxxxxxxxxxxxxxxxxxxxxxxxxxxxxxxxx

How to Cook:

1. Add the flour sugar and baking powder to a bowl and mix.

2. Pour in the milk and oil and mix.

3. Break in the egg and mix.

4. Add in vanilla essence and pour a tbsp. of the batter into lined cupcake molds.

5. Bake in a preheated 350 Fahrenheit oven for 30 minutes.

6. Serve warm.

Recipe 26: Danish Pastry

Chuck is often seen enjoying a lavish breakfast spread, with his parents. From fruit salads to crepes, the table is busy with a lot of food. One interesting part of the table is Danish Pastries, which look mouth-watering. You can follow this simple recipe.

Yield: 35

Total Prep Time: 2 hours

List of Ingredients:

- 10 oz. cream cheese
- 6 tbsp. sugar
- 2 tbsp. flour
- 1 tsp. vanilla extract
- 2 egg yolks
- 1 tbsp. water
- 1 pack puff pastry
- 10 tbsp. raspberry jam

xxxxxxxxxxxxxxxxxxxxxxxxxxxxxxxxxx

How to Cook:

1. Add yolks to a bowl with the water and whisk.

2. Place the puff pastry on a floured surface and roll it into 10-inch squares.

3. Place on a lined baking tray.

4. Add a tsp. of cream cheese on top of each square and a tsp. of jam.

5. Brush opposite ends of the pastry with the egg yolk and bring them together.

6. Brush the top with the egg mixture and bake in a preheated 425 Fahrenheit oven for 15 minutes.

7. Serve warm.

Recipe 27: Serena's Croissants

As mentioned, Serena is a big foodie and always hungry. Her favorite dessert has to be chocolate croissants, which she loves digging into.

Yield: 4

Total Prep Time: 40 minutes

List of Ingredients:

- 1 tbsp. water
- 1 sheet puff pastry
- 1 egg
- 2/3 cup chocolate chips

xxxxxxxxxxxxxxxxxxxxxxxxxxxxxxxxxxxxx

How to Cook:

1. Add the egg and water to a bowl and beat.

2. Add the pastry to a floured surface and roll out into a 16-inch square.

3. Cut them into 8 inch and 4-inch triangles and place the smaller ones over the bigger ones.

4. Add 2 tsp. of the chocolate chips in the center of each small triangle and roll them starting with the smaller ones followed by the bigger ones.

5. Brush each croissant with the egg mixture and bake in a preheated 350 Fahrenheit oven for 30 minutes.

6. Serve warm.

Recipe 28: Strawberries and Cream

I'm sure your mind traveled to Nate and Serena's intimate scene. As we know, Serena seductively eats strawberries and cream before her steamy session with Nate and does the same before her session with Dan. And why not! They are Aphrodisiacs after all.

Yield: 2

Total Prep Time: 10 minutes

List of Ingredients:

- 2 cups strawberries
- 1 cup whipping cream
- 5 tbsp. sugar
- 2 tsp. vanilla extract

xxxxxxxxxxxxxxxxxxxxxxxxxxxxxxxxxxxxx

How to Cook:

1. Wash the strawberries and cut them in half.

2. Sprinkle the sugar all over and let them sit for 5 minutes.

3. Whip the cream until stiff peaks form and refrigerate for an hour.

4. Add the strawberries to a plate and serve with a dollop of cream on the side.

Recipe 29: Madeline Cookies

In season 4, the gang goes to Paris and explores the beautiful country. Blair is seen having Madeleine cookies, which are native to the region. A cross between cookies and cake, they are delicious shell-shaped treats.

Yield: 12

Total Prep Time: 30 minutes

List of Ingredients:

- 1/3 cup sugar
- ½ cup flour
- 1 tbsp. lemon zest
- ¼ cup butter
- 2 eggs
- Powdered sugar to sprinkle

xxxxxxxxxxxxxxxxxxxxxxxxxxxxxxxxxxx

How to Cook:

1. Add the eggs and vanilla to a bowl and beat till light in texture.

2. Continue beating and add in the sugar.

3. Add in the flour and fold the mixture.

4. Add in the butter and lemon zest and beat.

5. Pour batter into shell-shaped molds and bake in a preheated 375 Fahrenheit oven for 15 minutes.

6. Add to a plate and sprinkle powdered sugar.

7. Serve with tea or coffee.

Recipe 30: Vanessa's Candies

Vanessa and Nate briefly date each other. On their first anniversary, Vanessa buys Nate a gift from a candy bar. Here's to Vanessa's gift!

Yield: 4-6

Total Prep Time: 30 minutes

List of Ingredients:

- 5 tbsp. cocoa powder
- 1 ½ cup milk powder
- 5 tbsp. unsalted butter
- 2/3 cup sugar
- ½ cup water

xxxxxxxxxxxxxxxxxxxxxxxxxxxxxxxxxxxx

How to Cook:

1. Heat water in a pan and add in the sugar.

2. Switch off the heat once the sugar reaches a syrup consistency.

3. Add in the butter and whisk.

4. Gradually add the cocoa powder and milk powder and mix till well combined.

5. Pour the mixture on to a greased plate and refrigerate for 30 minutes.

6. Use cookie cutters to cut the chocolates and serve.

Conclusion

There you have it. 30 dishes featured in your favorite drama show. Hope you have fun trying out the dishes and entertaining your friends.

Do not limit yourself to just these and switch around the ingredients to come up with your signature dishes.

Go on, hit the kitchen, cause a scandal and don't forget to have fun.

XOXO

Gossip Girl

Announcement

Thank you very much for getting this book. By buying my book you show me that you are ready to learn new skills and I can tell for sure you have made the best decision. I become a recipe writer because I love to share my knowledge and experience so that other people can learn.

What's even more special is that from all the books that are available on the internet today you have mine. With every purchase done it's like a gift to me, proof that I've made the best decision, turning my experience and knowledge into a book.

Still, please do not forget to leave feedback after reading the book. This is very important for me because I'll know how far I have reached. Even if you have any suggestions that you think it will make my future books even more practice please do share. Plus, everyone else that won't be able to decide which book to get next will have real feedback to read.

Thank you again

Your truly

Betty Green

About the Author

The one thing she loves more than cooking is eating. Yes, Betty Green enjoys tasting new dishes and loves to experiment with food. While sticking to the classics is also a thing, she wants to create recipes that people can enjoy daily.

She really understands the struggle of choosing the next lunch or dinner or what they should serve at their parties. So, she makes sure that her recipes are not only great for family dinners, or even a single dish but for parties too.

She always says "I have a strong sense of smell and taste, which gives me an advantage in creating new recipes from scratch".

The best part of Betty's recipes is that they are practical and very easy to make. When she does use ingredients that are not so easy to find or rarely used in cooking she makes sure to explain everything and add a simplified cooking description so that everyone can make them.

Everyone who got a cookbook from her says that she changed their life. Helped them finally enjoy spending time in the kitchen, which even helped them bond stronger with their family and friends.

Well, after all, food is one of the best ways to connect with people whether they make the dish together or they sit down and eat it. There are countless ways food can help you in your life, aside from keeping you fed and healthy.

Manufactured by Amazon.ca
Acheson, AB